Kingdom Come

The Miami University Press Poetry Series
General Editor: James Reiss

Kingdom Come

Jim Simmerman

Miami University Press
Oxford, Ohio

Library of Congress Cataloging-in-Publication Data

Simmerman, Jim,
    Kingdom come : poems / by Jim Simmerman.
        p. cm.
    ISBN 1-881163-26-1 (alk. paper). – ISBN 1-881163-27-X (alk.
paper)
    I. Title.
PS3569.I4726K56   1999
811'.54 – dc21
                                                        98-24829
                                                            CIP

The paper in this book meets the guidelines
for permanence and durability of the Committee
on Production Guidelines for Book Longevity
of the Council on Library Resources.♾

Printed in the U.S.A.

9 8 7 6 5 4 3 2 1

Acknowledgments

My thanks to the editors of the following publications, where poems herein first found readers:

Bloomsbury Review: "The Testament" (as "Will")

Bughouse: "The Messiah" (as "Flying")

Controlled Burn: "The Gospel" and "The Martyr"

5 AM: "The Judge"

Hayden's Ferry Review: "The Baptist" and "The Kingdom Come"

Laurel Review: "The Disciple" and "The Philistine"

Negative Capability: "The Brothers"

New England Review: "The Flood" (as "For Everything We Can't Put Down")

New Letters: "The Ascetic" and "The Psalmist"

Oxford Magazine: "The Haircut" and "The Magi"

Poetry: "The Monastic"

Poetry Miscellany: "The Christian Soldier" and "The Prophet"

Prairie Schooner: "The Angel," "The Sacrifice," and "The Wife"

Rocky Mountain Review of Language and Literature: "The Insurrectionist," "The Sinners," and "The Test"

"The Apostle," "The Miracle," and "The Paradise" appeared in the anthology *Fever Dreams: Contemporary Arizona Poetry,* University of Arizona Press, 1997.

"The Carpenter" appeared in the anthology *XY Files: Poems on the Male Experience,* Sherman Asher Publishing, 1997.

"The Lost" appeared in my chapbook *Yoyo,* GreenTower Press, 1994.

Thanks also to Hawthornden Castle and Northern Arizona University for supporting my work on these poems.

Contents

And he that sat upon the throne said, Behold, I make all things new. And he said unto me, Write:

– Revelations 21:5

The Old Testament

The Paradise

In retrospect, of course, it was all
predictable: how the tedium inherent
in perfection would make itself apparent
over time – which was ample. Once we

had sampled each permissible delicacy,
named each animal and strolled hand-
in-hand to the end of the garden path
and back a couple of million times,

we were prime candidates for anything
a little different, a little naughty
even, and for reasons it didn't take
a deity to divine. How many seasons –

though we never saw one leaf wither
and drop, never saw a single creature
curl into itself like a question mark
and expire – did we submit without

backtalk to the blatant humiliation
of being treated like children needing
constant supervision? We who had
arrived full-grown, and lacked in

consequence such memories as might
routinely assist another in whiling away
a restless night, suppressed entirely
our incredulity that *this* was paradise:

the same solemn song and dance forever
and ever; the utter frustration of living
with someone with whom you could neither
bicker nor neck, could never even begin

to rib nor discuss the rudiments of lust
and procreation – not knowing if they were
co-worker, sweetheart, sibling, or what . . . .

*For God doth
know that in the
day ye eat there-
of, then your eyes
shall be opened,
and ye shall be as
gods. . . .*
– Genesis 3:5

15

Who wouldn't apply for emigration?

Who wouldn't take a bite of temptation
just to taste its sweet, forbidden meat
and to feel its sticky juices sluice
down the throat and into the blood:

the sexual flood and flush of the body
abruptly awakened to its own nakedness,
the latent possibility of every nook
and cranny made manifest at last –

albeit our blushes were mistaken
for shame . . . . And when we came
through the gate we felt like kids
on a date, unchaperoned, nervous,

but ready and willing, whatever
the price of ditching the garden
to rut through the wilderness . . . .
By way of goodbye, we mooned paradise.

The Wife

When we were leaving the city
I was nagged by a feeling of
having somehow forgotten something –

a small but persistent itching
somewhere in the middle of the back
of the brain, where memory couldn't

reach a finger to scratch it;
and where, if I'd had eyes there,
I would have seen what it was

I wasn't to return to and about
which, now, there seemed nothing
I could do. You know: a door

unlocked, a candle unsnuffed, some-
place or one to which I hadn't
said goodbye . . . . I, who knew better

than most the trials of marriage
to a trusting man, one who was wont
to consult freely with angels and

strangers alike, and who believed –
oh gullible darling! – the least
likely of rumors murmured in taverns,

and who was given to panic and visions
of doom. Soon enough we would have
found a room in a different city

with a different name, found ourselves
amid new friends with whom we could
complain about the blasphemies

and evils that walk the streets
of the world like sullen immigrants . . . .

*And when the
morning arose, then
the angels hastened
Lot, saying, Arise,
take thy wife, and
thy two daughters,
which are here; lest
thou be consumed
in the iniquity of
the city.*
– Genesis 19:15

17

And it would be the same. It

would be time's way of recording and
playing itself back ad infinitum –
the good of which I just couldn't see,

no matter that it would have been
an easy enough, a wifely thing
to do for the man I loved and

even honored, but whom I could
not, finally, obey. To this day
I pray he never learns what, but

for his blind obedience and trust,
would have been obvious all along:
I simply walked away – turned

back to a city with a home and a family
that needed looking after. Such
was my lot, for which I was unnamed.

The Sacrifice

I liked the kid but the voice
ricocheting round in my head
like a hard foul ball in a

batting cage said, "Damn it
all, Abe, what's the matter
with you? Don't you want to

be called to the big leagues
some day? Maybe pinch hit
for the Angels? Who knows,

maybe even start with the Padres?
Say, you could be another Jesus
Alou if you'd just learn to con-

centrate: eye on ball and all
that jazz – get it? – and clean
the cowflop out of your ears,

OK?! When I say step up and take
a cut you'd best let me see you
swinging away. You're blessed,

hell yes, with a stroke that's clean
as a cherub's butt, but you've
got to get the lead out – move it!

I mean – if you want to be safe.
The main thing is, don't think
so much: that's management stuff

and you're paid to play. So
knock off the backtalk and mind
games, Einstein, and get your head

back into the game. You need
to learn to read the signs.

*And Abraham
stretched forth his
hand, and took
the knife to slay
his son.*
– Genesis 22:10

19

Look: *this* means pull it;

this means take; and *this*
means lay it on the line,
means *sacrifice* for God's sake!"

The Angel

That was only my ring name of course:
  a little something to entice the crowd,
like the silver singlet with wings
embroidered on the back that I wore
along with a shimmery, haloed cowl.

*And Jacob was left
alone; and there
wrestled a man with
him until the break-
ing of the day.*
– Genesis 32:24

I was proud of my work, such as it was:
to be the worthy opponent of those
chosen to climb their way up the ladder
of fame – though for reasons that were
never entirely clear to me, unless

it's that kismet or charisma or kissing
ass will get you farther in the world
of wrestling than cunning, skill, and grace.
Of which I had plenty – practicing moves
until I could perform them in my sleep

or, for that matter, anyone else's;
perfecting holds from which you'd need
a corporate attorney to escape; dieting,
lifting, abstaining from booze and sex.
My motto was ever, "Whatever it takes."

Although I was never given the breaks,
it's said I attained a certain following
among a few aficionados of the game
who admired my inimitable flying leaps
from somewhere well above the top rope,

my signature hip lock, the way I ate pain.
Still, who can blame me the little bitterness
I retain like the aftertaste of asparagus?
For to many, most, I would always remain
chump-change, palooka, charlatan, bum –

the one who took a dive in the final fall
of a championship match with an upstart

21

too weak to pin a slip. Given my image,
what choice did I have? I honored
my contract, stuck wholly to the script.

The Brothers

_L_ike we were the wicked step-
  sisters in the Cinderella saga . . . .
Not. Though to hear it told

we were lower than dirt, covetous,
conniving. Worse: crude ancillaries
in a plot concocted by a pathological

paranoid for the purpose of advancing
his own career . . . . Always steer clear
of braggadocio and flashy fashion,

our father advised us, who had
always been partial to our brother
Joseph; and yet – go figure! –

gave him that pricy, preposterous
getup in which he looked – no
other way to put it – like a dime-

store pimp with a line up his nose.
Why he chose to cruise the streets
each night, consorting with heaven

only knows what unsavory company,
dragging his wasted butt into bed
each morning after the rest of us

had already left for work was pure
mystery. But when the day arrived
he didn't return, we were *worried.*

Indeed, we took emergency leave
from our jobs, without pay, hurried
out and away to look for the boy

who might have strayed into bonafide
trouble this time, bitten off more

*And it came to
pass, when Joseph
was come unto his
brethren, that they
stripped Joseph out
of his coat, his
coat of many colors
that was on him;
And they took him,
and cast him into
a pit . . . .*
– Genesis 37:23-24

23

of the hard core than he could chew,

but who – albeit he'd made mistakes –
was first, last, ever our brother . . . .
Why even bother rebutting a story

that has been so thoroughly, lop-
sidedly covered by now it might
as well be gospel? No reason;

no reason at all. Though we know
what we know. Facts are facts.
You can believe it or not, but

if he would just come back home
and ask us to, we would still
give him the shirts off our backs.

The Haircut

*W*as that a raindrop or is God
spitting on me? Since I got
my haircut I can't see shit
or shinola. Delilah, you
bitch, I can't believe you

snitched on me and the tint-free
roots of my power. Where are you
anyway in your life that you're
so soured and fed up with men
you'd just as soon bust your

husband as not? Are you lesbo
or what? I just want to know
before I go out on a limb
of lunacy forever. Never again
will I trust a dame; never

again strain myself on behalf
of a brother. Why bother? Other,
weaker men have been blessed
for the faith they professed
to hoard under a bushel – all

sackcloth and trash talk. Me,
I knock in the noggins of a
couple of thousand Philistines
with the jawbone of an ass
just to pass a single hour

in the favor of my Father and
what's my reward? – to wind up
blind, scalped, and hogtied;
divided from country; minus
a wife; bullied and baited

like a bear or a boar. Where
are those famous pillars of
the temple said to be sturdy

*And Samsom said
unto the lad that
held him by the
hand, Suffer me
that I may feel the
pillars whereupon
the house standeth,
that I may lean
upon them.*
– Judges 16:26

and pretty as the legs of a
goddess? I just want to rest

between them a minute; I just
want that small satisfaction,
who once was a guy any woman
would fall for and all – give me
strength, Lord! – affirmative action.

The Philistine

Though I had always been large
   for my age, I was never one
to pick a fight; never went out

for competitive sports or bullied
my way to the front of the line.
If mine was the girth and height

of a Titan, I felt like a schoolgirl
inside, would blush at the rush
of my classmates to recess – whose

horseplay and roughneck I could
not abide. Believe me, I tried
and tried to make friends, but

my smile capsized in the sea
of my jowls; my pass at a laugh
howled forth like a gale. Sometimes

I frightened myself. Sometimes
I felt I'd been issued in error
a body I could not return;

could not get out of, shrink, or
take in. Whatever I did, I grew . . . .
When I was drafted they threw me

up to the front, promoted me solely
based on my size; and for the way
I could make the enemy quake, turn

tail, and flee just by waving
my arms and rolling my eyes – an act
I devised by pretending to dance,

though of course I had never been
asked. I was lonely as ever,

And David put his
hand in his bag,
and took thence a
stone, and slang it,
and smote the
Philistine . . . .
   – I. Samuel 17:49

even with rank; my duty was easy,

but crass . . . . Until that son
of a shepherd – a child, really,
with the voice of an alto, skin

like milk, eyes of cornflower
blue – called me out to the field
of battle at last, as if

onto the floor of a ballroom . . . .
And when the rock hit my head
it felt like a kiss. What had I

ever wanted but love? To be swept
off my feet completely, just once?
Oh, David, my hero, my dove!

The Psalmist

The ad on the scroll said, "Wanted:
your original song lyrics and poems
to set to music. Established firm

*And David
spake unto the Lord
the words of this
song . . . .*
– II. Samuel 22:1

representing legendary artist seeks
new talent for possible collaboration.
Over 2,000 years in the industry."

So I sent in the application card
which guaranteed me professional
assessment of my work, for which

I would be charged a modest fee
refundable in full so long as
the work was accepted, recorded,

entered the charts with a bullet;
went gold, went platinum with
overseas sales; garnered the artist

a Grammy. See: I was a simple man
with limited prospects, a hillbilly
really, who didn't know a psalm

from a sow. Like my daddy, I worked
hard in the fields, living on cold tack
and sleeping at night with the animals.

But right along I had these dreams
of a better life where I would dwell
in a custom home with indoor plumbing,

my cup full, a table prepared –
all those wonders I had seen once
in a catalogue in an outhouse . . . .

So I sent in this country thing
I had written about green pastures,

29

valleys, goodness and such: not

much, but it came from the heart
and I guess some people could relate
because the rest, you know, is history.

I was *chosen* and it could happen
to you. But you must act fast.
Please sign and return *immediately*.

The Judge

Disappointment is the psychological
recipe with which we blame others
for our own errors in judgment . . . .
That's what I was thinking when

they called me into court to
adjudicate the dispute between
two women, each claiming to be
mother of the same baby – unsavory,

half-baked soap opera stuff.
To remain emotionally detached
is the job of a judge; further,
to nudge, via intellect and

propriety, the jalapeño
huff of innuendo and flagrant
allegation toward some level
table where justice is served

coolly – the soothing sorbet
in a five-alarm meal. What harm,
I thought at first, can there be
in a ruling of joint custody?

Aren't two mothers, de facto,
better than one? What daughter
or son wouldn't benefit from
a double helping of maternal love?

And what mother, given a choice,
wouldn't rejoice in splitting
the pangs of parenting – not to
mention the cooking, cleaning,

and laundry? But women can be
ornery. I could, after a time,
see that they were having none

*And the King said,
Divide the living
child in two, and
give half to the one,
and half to the
other.*
    – I. Kings 3:25

31

of my sage counsel; my legendary

fairness was a hairnet to the bald.
I was appalled, angry, fed up to here,
frankly, with the disappointing
goulash being made of jurisprudence.

And though my verdict would be
likened unto the pièce de résistance
of a master chef, I confess:
my passions overruled my head.

I meant what I said about cleaving
the squirt . . . . Hell, would have
done it myself just to close
the case and dish out the just deserts.

The Test

"This is a test; this is only a test . . . . "
Let me tell you about my God: Mr.
Do-Unto-Others who did unto me
what I wouldn't do unto a dog;

Mr. Boil, Mr. Smite, Mr. Negative
Reinforcement – for whom I rolled over,
sat up, and fetched like each
of his dropkicks was horsemeat;

like each of the hot licks he beat
on my skull was a baffling pat
of affection. What did I do to deserve
what I got from my Lord, Mr. Pro-

vivisection? Where did I err
in obedience school that my staying
and heeling were flunked, that my
reverent yip of praise was assayed

as the snarl of a quarrelsome mutt?
What rug did I wet? What scroll
did I trash to be scolded and lashed
to a tree around which I became so wound

its bark took a bite out of me?
See: my only aim was to please;
in pleasing, to worship the strange
Mr. Just, who giveth and taketh

away what he gave according to
ground rules I couldn't dig up.
Wouldn't dig up, as Jehovah's
my witness, who watches me

constantly cringe in his fields,
alert to the slightest flight
of his glance, the terrible dance

33

of his thunderous heels. If meat

is the matter, my bone on his
platter. If sacrifice, here,
my belly I bare. If fealty,
look at me pointing impeccably,

almost an effigy, ear ever cocked
for the voice of my Master, Mr.
Disaster, to vouchsafe my pass
through his storm and his dark.

The New Testament

The Carpenter

Someone nailed her; and someone
would have to marry her, who
yet maintained she was a virgin –

mercy! – what with her belly bulging
like barrel staves. Still, she was
a cutie: her bright eyes shining

like varnished mahogany, her skin
golden as honey oak. Finally, I spoke
plainly to her, as befits a man

of my trade, saying, "Sweetie,
you have snapped a chalk line
down the center of my heart,

cut through it cleanly; won't you
finish your work and be my wife?"
Which was a hard row from the git-go,

what with taxes and the necessary
commuting to construction sites;
plus there were the predictable

sniggers and jokes about another
man's chisel in my toolbox . . . .
But we managed. We survived.

And when the child arrived I
raised him as if he were my own,
instructed him in the many things

a carpenter should know: first
and last, good wood from bad;
how there's a time to sand

and a time to caulk; the wisdom
of working *with* the grain;

*Then Joseph being
raised from sleep
did as the angel of
the Lord had bid-
den him, and took
unto him his wife:
And knew her not
till she had
brought forth her
firstborn son . . . .
– Matthew 1:24-25*

that every job must stop. Sad

to say, his aptitude was minimal,
his interest in the family business
nil. Instead, he read, brooded,

roamed the wilderness alone –
a sensitive boy, and bright, but
looking for god-knows-what. I don't.

Frankly, it worried the wife awhile.
Frankly, it worried me too. Though
isn't that just the way of the young,

needing to figure it out on their own,
anything beating the old man's shoes?
Times were changing fast, it's true:

timber was scarcer; money tight. So
why not a future in fasting and prayer?
No chip off this block, the kid could be right.

The Magi

Truth to tell it was one long haul,
what with just one star to shine
the way – no road signs, no rest stops,
the sky all clouded up often as not . . . .

And what was there to do all day?
It would be a long time before
anyone invented the compass;
longer still before anyone received,

as a Christmas stocking-stuffer,
a deck of cards. Those camels
got pretty good mileage, it's true,
but who wouldn't long for an am/

fm radio-cassette with Dolby
and surround sound, a/c, cruise-
control, the whole nine yards
human desire, like a tape measure,

would stretch to eventually?
Though we wouldn't be around
to see it. We were three
weary travelers in a country

not our own. We didn't know
the language, didn't know the ways
the world can turn itself inside out
on its own like a sock in a dryer;

nor what ills might be visiting
themselves on friends and family
back home . . . .   Home, that land
we thought we might never get

back to. Home, that place from
which we were so far gone –
and this before the telephone,

*Now when Jesus
was born in
Bethlehem of Judea
in the days of
Herod the king,
behold, there came
wise men from the
east . . . .*
– Matthew 2:1

the postcard – the very memory

of it began to flicker out
like that fabled star we shadowed
without much remark. And though
we would go down in history

as kings, we were functionaries,
truth to tell. We had a job
to do and didn't ask questions.
Just saddled up and rode on in the dark.

The Disciple

Do this. Don't do that . . . . It's getting
pretty old, this sitting at the feet
of the celebrated Prince of Peace –

who gives us little – like a dog
begging a bone. I remember back home
I had a steady job in food services

with management potential, a rent-
controlled tent with a view, the kids
and wife to nag me if I needed that . . . .

But threw it all away as they say,
and not for some blond bimbo
with bodacious hooters and a tight ass.

No, it was just my luck to go
for the old I-will-make-you-
a-fisher-of-men bit – swallow it

hook, line, and sinker. Sometimes
I can't help but wonder where
else I might be today if I had

just tossed a couple of coppers
into the collection hat, said "thanks
but no thanks," and been on my John

Q. Public way . . . . Another thing:
those parables. I just don't get it
about the lilies of the field,

or what kind of rocket scientist
would build his house on sand,
or why, anyway, you'd want to stuff

a camel through the eye of a needle.
People are starting to look at me

*Peter answered him
and said, Lord, if it
be thou, bid me
come unto thee
on the water.*
   – Matthew 14:28

41

funny. I can't recall my last

hot meal. Sometimes he wanders away
for days like a cat that doesn't
give a damn, leaving us to stare

at our feet and mumble. Understand,
I'm not usually one to complain;
but what if someone told *you* to walk

on water? I know the bay's closed
to swimmers and boats. It's not
my fault. I'm just following orders.

The Miracle

First I was dead, then – *presto!* –
I wasn't. But like the lovely
and trusted assistant in a magic
show, I was not in a position to
disclose how the trick was done.

One thing though: you come back
fuzzy, addled, a tad bleary-eyed
from the other side of the curtain.
Another: there are still bills
to pay, some overdue. For certain

members of the audience, the ones
who had known and lived with you,
comes a catalogue of confusions:
the wife unwidowed, made to roll
back to her own side of the bed;

the child who had already mentally
spent his share of the inheritance
a little sullen, a little grudging.
Judging by the looks on the faces
of others, there was a fair amount

of skepticism running like an under-
current through the crowd; in lieu
of *bravos*, only a polite patty-cake
of applause . . . . No one had shown me
the clause in the contract permitting

death, if not completely satisfied,
to return me within thirty days.
And no one would ever understand
the ostracism I was to suffer in
consequence: the ways passersby

would wrinkle their noses and wince
at the aroma of my presence, that
rancid reek I could never entirely

*And when he thus
had spoken, he
cried with a loud
voice, Lazarus,
come forth. And he
that was dead came
forth....*
    – John 11:43-44

43

wash away; and the fey wrist-wags
of the vaguely amused, as if to say

in sign language, "Now isn't that
just the quaintest thing?" –
insensitive bastards, every one.
And while it's yet true my days
are numbered, the pagination now

is hopelessly skewed – like reading
a book in which you've already looked
at the final chapter: a tale entitled
The Miracle, referring not to the act
but to the fact that anyone bothered.

The Apostle

What would you have done, times
   being what they were? – no drive-ins,
no Gameboys, no karaoke or TV;

*And we are his
witnesses of these
things . . . .*
   – Acts 5:32

only the interminable national pastime
of tossing heretics to the lions –
the outcome of which was predictable,

and for which, anyway, it was impossible
to get tickets unless you knew someone.
Day out, day in: casting lots and whatall,

resoling your sandals, abiding your flock;
occasionally, maybe, getting lucky
enough to do a little begetting.

Mostly not. Mostly it was ghostly quiet
and, frankly, boring living in B.C. –
though we didn't know to call it that –

waiting for somebody to do something
newsworthy enough for us to get cranking
on the invention of a new calendar

where we could start X-ing off the dates
until some new holiday we could not yet
imagine how to celebrate rolled around.

Mostly we were desperate unto dudgeon
for a new look, a new sound – anything
to distract us from the whittling

of sticks into smaller sticks
our lives had not so rapidly become.
So when some guy blows into town

honking and preaching the *new* religion,
laying down the *new* law

45

like an ace-high straight, telling it

def like a double shot of Motown
in an after-hours juke joint,
what could I do but enlist?

What could I do but throw up my hands,
kick back my chair, and dance
into the future tuned to

Can I get a witness? Yes! Lordy yes!

The Sinners

We were all players. We were all pimps,
punks, tricks, or whores. Even the beggars
with their homemade stumps and sores self-
inflicted were on the grift; even the poor,

whose angle it was to tangle themselves
inextricably in the sticky web of the streets,
feeding off the trickle-down of table scraps
and cracked bones: for the truly hungry,

easy meat. Sweet pickings also for scribes
and Pharisees, fattening their coffers on
bribes and the tithing of marks made brute-
stupid in their hearkening to fixed verdicts

and false decrees rolled out daily like
loaded dice. As for me, it was my fortune
and privilege to lead the double-life
of the well-endowed; to be, at once,

the proud and proper daughter of one whose
patronage and renown permitted his hand
ample access to the pocket of the state,
and to be – at my pleasure, and far from

the halls of my father – the archangel
of the city's night: stark and radiant
Salome. Though expensive, I was free
with my favors once purchased. Men were

born again in my bed. Marriages dead
for years were resuscitated by the mouth-
to-mouth I applied, the delicate tunes
I blew into the reeds of the husbands,

the carnal cartography in which I schooled
the wives. I thrived on desire and the fires
I kindled, if not without cost, blazed

*But when Herod's
birthday was kept,
the daughter of
Herodias danced
before them, and
pleased Herod.
Whereupon he
promised with an
oath to give her
whatsoever she
would ask. And
she, being before
instructed of her
mother, said, Give
me here John
Baptist's head in a
charger.*
    – Matthew 14:6-8

47

like miracles in the cold temples

of the appointed, their loins anointed
with the oils of their lust. Who did not
seek me out among those born of woman?
Priests and prophets I held in my arms,

taught them to pray to the sway of my hips
while my lips stole them wholly away
from their gods. Even the smug one who
chastened my mother, the self-proclaimed

baptist, paid me a call, making me promise
to keep his name secret in exchange for
the promise of untold reward. "From my Lord,"
he said, winking an eye as he took me –

the bastard – for free, deprived me of what
was rightfully mine in accordance with law
and the custom of thieves. His deceit,
I have to admit, was sweet: a confidence

game for heaven's sake. I could have forgiven
his quick spurt of passion for a piece
of the action, a cut of the take. "Make
me an offer," I said to him later. "Show me

the face of your Lord." Silent, he looked
first into, then through me – his eyes like
cast stones – and I knew him for what he was:
a sinner like me, but so blessed with success

he had come to believe his own con; had
feasted so well on the belly of the beast
he had come to begrudge his image in others,
and so to judge us for picking the bones.

So be it. But I had my own bone to pick:
you get what you pay for or vice-versa.
He was just a John to whom I gave head –
his own with its cheap smirk of virtue.

The Insurrectionist

I copped a plea, was permitted to go
free for reasons I did not care
to understand. I – who'd murdered,

maimed, molested, had a hand in
every pocket in the province – walked,
then ran like spillage, fast, away

from that place of trial by trumpery
and traducement; cast no backward glance
at the man made to take up his cross and

dance the clumsy two-step of the framed . . . .
What was his name, whose crime was talk
and a certain predilection for self-

bemusement? And what was the bounty
worth ratting him out? In the short
spell we shared a cell I got to know him

not at all, save in the way one gets
to know the doomed for what they are:
the unintelligible mutterings that drip

from their lips like soup scud, how
their eyes roll back as if to stare
at some mural painted on the inside

of the skull . . . . No, it wasn't fair
that I – who had a rap sheet a cubit long
and not a prayer of rehabilitation –

should skate on that date when custom
required of the public one gesture
of mercy, however forced or ill-advised.

Nor was it long before the authorities
realized their mistake: to make

Therefore
when they were
gathered together,
Pilate said unto
them, Whom will
ye that I release
unto you?
Barabbas, or Jesus
which is called
Christ?
    – Matthew 27:17

49

of a mild man a martyr, then a legend

that would sink its teeth into the very
throat of history . . . . And me? I got
back to business as usual, but with

a new-found respect for participatory
democracy and a genuine fondness
for a system of justice which may be

blind, but is not dumb. "Give us
Barabbas," bleated the sheep . . . .
Got what they asked for and then some.

The Messiah

They take my ticket
and let me board the plane.
They ask me to buckle
my safety belt and

do I want a drink.
What they don't know
won't hurt them
won't do me any good

is my experience.
This is what I think:
I can eat the food
and sip the wine

and watch the in-flight movie.
I can smile at the girl
with the Easter basket
across the aisle

and see how pretty
and hopeful she is.
I can close my eyes
and stare at the stone

that won't roll away
from the cave of my skull.
And then? And then
we're permitted to land.

They let me deplane
and claim my cross
and walk back into the world
like anyone else.

The thing is, I'm dead.
I've always been dead.
I've always been dying
to tell you myself.

My God, my God,
why hast thou for-
saken me?
– Mark 15:34

51

Kingdom Come

The Kingdom Come

Did I sell my soul to write
these lines? I don't know,
but can already imagine a day
of fire, flood, brimstone,

Thy kingdom come.
Thy will be done . . .
– Matthew 6:10

and judgment, when the Holy
P.A. will rumble and quake
like a voice from the void,
thunder out my name, call me

thus to the office of the Supreme
Headmaster, who will shake
his head sadly, sigh, and say –
with something like patience

at the end of its chain –
"Does this belong to you?"
as he lifts from his desk
what you hold in your hand . . . .

For which I will make no
excuse, nor lamely attempt
to lay blame on another, but
stare him square in his all-

seeing eye, make him blink
if I can – like trying to
wink the moon and the stars
from the heavens – and reply:

I was made in the image
of the Maker, Your Honor,
dropped dumb and without
syllabus into the classroom

of my life; lacking lunch
money, prerequisites, and
with the attention span of

a triceratops, nonetheless,

applied myself as best I could;
my attendance was perfect.
Besides, can you not recall,
Your Omniscientness, what

it was like to feel so bored
and strange and alone you
began to doodle, make things
up, take an interest in them

and where they might go? If
not, then show me no mercy,
Your Wrathfulness; lay it on
hard with lash and tongue,

crown me with the dunce cap of
the held back by circumstance,
deliver me from commencement
and the pomp of kingdom come.

The Gospel

Heaven's lousy with guitars no one plays.
The music's too raucous and anyhow,
how to hook the straps around the wings?

On one hairy acid trip I died
and went to heaven, only heaven turned
out to be the same as where I'd been.

Heaven turned out to be a tabloid banner
you could euthanize time goofing on
in any supermarket checkout line:

ROCK'N'ROLL MUSIC TRANSMITS GOVERNMENT
SECRETS TO U.F.O.'S. EVIDENCE
PROVES ELVIS DESCENDANT OF CHRIST.

Evidence proves heaven really exists
in the shopping carts of the homeless,
the suicide hotline, the A.A. singles' dance.

Evidence proves heaven is where they dress you
in the clean smock of the lunatic, take away
your pets and Percocet, take away your hands. . . .

This is the gospel according to man,
according to portents and MTV.
This is the gospel as writ in the fuzz-

tone feedback of a Fender, November, dosed
and orbiting the walls of America
like some strung-out Joshua beamed to A.D.

where A.D. stands for "acute disorder"
or "abject despair" or "already dead";
where the state performs its mandatory

drum solo against the ribs of the poor;
where the invisible strings that hold up

57

the body begin to tangle and shred;

and where further miracles of heaven
on earth amass like power chords that
blast through the mist: the dead raised

to public office, the infirm made to take up
their beds and walk, spit rubbed into the eyes
of the blind, the laying on of fists . . . .

The Ascetic

It's like the old joke where you go
to the doctor and say, "Doctor, it hurts
when I do this," and the doctor says,
"Don't do that." Only this is no joke.

This is the way I'm learning to pray
ceaselessly to the God of mind-
your-manners, learning to trim
the fat of the flesh from the meat

of the soul. Like any good butcher,
I'm getting to know the intimate
details of anatomy and the value
of a sharp knife. In my former life

I worshiped comfort and, if not joy,
certainly the absence of pain.
I could borrow, say, the spiritual
equivalent of a cup of sugar

from the squeals of the contestants
on "Wheel of Fortune." I could sink
into the naugahyde of the La-Z-Boy
recliner so deeply sometimes it seemed

some miracle of transubstantiation,
seemed I had *become* the recliner
in the way that those Chee-tos
I had eaten earlier as a bedtime snack

had become, inexplicably, me.
So: La-Z-Boy, Chee-tos, game show of
the brain – trinity to which I sacrificed
nothing because it was not required,

and because I was permitted to dream
of the Holy Cities of the Princess
Cruise Line and the Epcot Center

*But I keep under
my body, and
bring it into
subjection . . . .*
– I. Corinthians 9:27

59

into which, one day, I might be received . . . .

But this was false prophecy. This
was the trick the fox played on the hare:
a tar-baby La-Z-Boy theology
into which you can sink so deeply

you'll never get out without giving up
a little fur, a little hide . . . .   And
that is why I abide these bottle caps
in the bottoms of my slippers, this

frayed electrical extension cord
wound tightly around my chest,
the ice cubes I swallow whole . . . .
And that is how what began

as a joke can end in a prayer
where you go to the Lord and say,
"Lord, it hurts when I do this."
And the Lord says, "Good."

The Christian Soldier

It's hard to fight the Devil
when the battlefield is Hell.
This I know – having girded
my loins with rightousness

*Thou therefore
endure hardness, as
a good soldier of
Jesus Christ.*
  – II. Timothy 2:3

instead of asbestos, having
armed myself with a hymnal
when what I needed was a hose.
What I needed was the Holy Ghost

to radio in an air strike:
a squadron of angelic bombers
flying in the formation of
the Cross overhead. What I

needed was the dead champions
of the Old Testament (Joshua,
David, Sampson, and so on)
resurrected and ready to rumble . . . .

A humble do-gooder and chronic
bumbler, I was much amazed to
be responsible for the outcome
of the grudge match between

Good and Evil (the dark side
is powerful indeed), but agreed
in principle to the merits of
the meek; was much impressed by

the girth of the purse I'd inherit
(the very Earth!) should I emerge
victorious, still able to stand
upright on my own two feet . . . .

How sweet is the plum plucked
from the highest branch of
the Teflon tree of adversity!

And how insanely mixed are

the metaphors marching through
the brain drained of everything
but adrenalin and feeble one-
liners rhymed to time the boot

thumps advancing on the fray . . . .
Nevermind that the fat lady
didn't sing that day – the fat
lady's taking voice lessons

and will be back (guaranteed)
by the time I've licked my
wounds into scars. Thus it is
written: *Best two out of three.*

The Prophet

I was taught that the body is home
to the Father, whose house has many rooms.
But also that whosoever would dwell
in the house of the Father must abandon
the body. Frankly, I was confused.

*A prophet is not
without honor, save
in his own country,
and in his own
house.*
    – Matthew 13:57

Frankly, I couldn't see where –
followed to anything like a logical
conclusion – the metaphor was headed.
Not home, unless home is a funhouse
of trick mirrors and tilted floors

where things appear to roll uphill
and the doors are tinier than you
suspected. Still, I pledged,
if selected to head the Holy
Commission on Relocation, to find

the blueprints to the promised abode
where we should all be admitted like
lucky orphans; pledged to inspect
the wiring and the plumbing and
see that things were up to code . . . .

For a long time – longer than Moses –
I roamed through many strange lands
and foreign dreams, rode the bus
through many bad neighborhoods
in search of the place I could almost

taste the memory of in advance.
What chance did I have, lacking faith
or a road map? And what sad idols
had been erected in my absence?
The past tense gets you only so far.

What I needed was a car with a full
tank, a little Jesus on the dashboard,
the radio dialed to an all-night

63

gospel station. What I needed was
a nation of Sunday-go-to-meeting

neighbors to tail through the wilderness
of streets, strip malls, and unmowed yards,
to lead me to the golden porch light
shining down upon the "welcome" mat . . . .
Though it turns out I was in charge.

And though it turns out I didn't do half
a bad job for someone who couldn't
find shit with his ass. I was lost,
but finally found the way home – into
which I am now not permitted to pass.

The Lost

You know how it is: Cold. Dark.
    You're lost and getting loster
somewhere out there in the Posthumous
Boot Camp for Spiritual Retards –

you and the rocks and the skittish
rodents whose mission it is
to live in terror and die in private
and whose squeaks are code-talk

for "Hey Soldier, catch a clue."
I do. Once, I threw a rock at the moon,
wanting to smash its face – that smugness –
out of the sky, wanting to fly

like a hoodlum balloon slapped
around by the wind for nothing
but the palm-flat *thwap* of it –
like in a cartoon they'd show

every Sunday in the burn ward of Hell . . . .
Which got me where? So far
as I can tell, this hanging fire
is harder: bushwhacking your way back

through places you thought you knew
like the taste of your own tongue;
laced into a pair of wasted boots;
packing a flashlight lacking a bulb

and a single inscrutable map;
asking yourself the same, lame
insubordinate questions to which
you've always suspected the answers:

Why am I lost? *Because.*
When will they look for me? *Never.*
How much longer do I have to go
on like this? *Longer. Forever.*

And the smoke
of their torment
ascendeth up for
ever and ever: and
they have no rest
day nor night . . . .
– Revelations 14:11

65

The Monastic

I said, I will
take heed to my
ways, that I sin
not with my
tongue: I will
keep my mouth
with a bridle....
   – Psalms 39:1

By now I've read so much of the text
of the theology of reclusion –
studying it like an eye chart
on which there's always one more
smaller, less legible line –

and choked back so many prayers –
they seem by now to leak
out the corner of my mouth
shrink-wrapped in bubbles
like comic book blab – you'd think

someone would have thought
to declare me patron saint
of dumb ideas and dead ends,
fashioned a little amulet
in my likeness to dangle

from the necks of the terminally
clueless and the cracked
rearview mirrors of junked cars;
you'd think someone by now
would have circled a square

in my honor on a calendar
devoid of numbers – a sort of secret
admirer's gift the amnesiac
keeps surprising himself with –
to commemorate the date

on which I stopped listening
to anyone but myself, stopped
talking to anyone but myself,
stopped talking and listening
even to myself finally and –

no one will remember this –
slipped from the fingers

of the world like soap –
amscrayed, lickety-split,
like that – taking with me

nothing but the echo of a hand
slapped flat on calm water
and the famous smirk the monastic
wears like a "kick me" sign
on his face, leaving behind nothing

but the hand and the water
and the cheap perfume of words
for which one acquires
first a tolerance, then a craving:
and that is how I have come

like a cave-in to this place
of mute worship and self-
rectitude, this monastery
I built by stacking one brick
of silence atop another –

mortaring them with the phlegm
that accrued in my throat
all these years like medicine
I was made to take, refused
to swallow – and in which I live

sparely according to the model
of the oyster and the snail –
those little apostles of peace
and privacy, those delicacies
martyred for nothing but their taste.

The Martyr

But when they
deliver you up, take
no thought of how
or what ye shall
speak . . . .

– Matthew 10:19

They say I was aloof but professional,
  in the manner of beasts which –
knowing no better or lacking choice –
file docilely into the slaughteryard.

They say it didn't smell good.
If you were there you would have had
to elbow your way through the mob
of rubbernecks and well-wishers

to get close enough to see the vein
in the side of my neck begin to
squirm like a salted slug; would
have had to vault the fence

in front of the stage and slide
a sawbuck into the vest pocket
of the honcho security thug to
get almost near enough to hear

the prayer I prayed with my lips
standing still, ventriloquist-style,
the whole while they were piling
around my ankles the brush and broken

contracts and bad reviews; would
have had to assist the stage crew
with the pouring on of kerosene
before you could even begin

to dream what it's like to be
up there – how the nerves stampede
when the house lights dim and
the crowd stumbles hush and

everyone's looking at no one
but you. Then the lighters flick on . . . .
They say I was hot; they say
I was cooking: all I could do.

The Testament

I leave my books to the blind,
   my records to the deaf,

my guitar and power tools to amputees.
I leave my car to the man

most often convicted
of drunk and reckless driving.

I leave my elbows, knees,
and orthopedic bills to be divied

among athletes who never got signed.
As for my mind,

I leave it to the sane:
let *them* lose it for a change.

To dreamers I leave my insomnia.
To the poor, my pockets

stuffed with lint.
To science, my poems.

My organs to the nonperforming arts.
To my ex-loves, all four of them,

I leave a fortune
in unlovely memories.

I leave the keys to the house
to a pond in the woods.

The house I leave
to matches and wind.

I leave my enemies my friends.

*For where a
testament is,
there must also
of necessity be
the death of the
testator.*
   – Hebrews 9:16

My smart remarks I leave to mimes,

mutes, mutts, and mustard seed.
I leave my clocks to the rocks,

my shoes to the trees,
my hats to the elk

whose bodies are closets.
I leave to my future

landlords, the meek, the unturned
cheek of me: damage deposit.

The Baptist

That was my job title, but I don't
   know. Mostly I felt like a man
unsure of his mission or calling
in a world gone inexplicably gaga

I indeed
baptize you
with water unto
repentance . . . .
   – Matthew 3:11

over the latest fad. Not so bad
as tattooing of course, that
permanent, sad, cartoonish art
which, given the dissolute acts

of my past, I eschewed – ever
paranoid of identifying marks.
Nor body-piercing, another pop
and pointless preoccupation among

the congregations of certain
sects who seemed not to feel
as though they had enough holes
in their heads already. Steady

most days, clean and sober, I tried
hard not to think about the brink
of ruination I teetered on always,
the tightwire of nerves between null

and void I tiptoed along. Was I
wrong then to pursue a vocation
the nature of which was commercial,
and for which the only requisites

were a knack for rhetoric and water?
Sacrosanct, self-employed, I blessed
each man, woman, son, and daughter
willing to cough up a quarter for

the privilege of having their heads
dunked under . . . . Until a day came
I discovered I had begun to hold

71

first one, then another, beneath

the surface a little longer; had
begun to take a sort of pleasure
in the way their faces clenched
against the pressure of my palm,

and in the twitchings and shudders
of the body possessed abruptly
by the holy spirit of its own
mortality, the pure chemical rush

of the brain to stake its claim
on the thin air of this earth . . . .
So high was I by then on the power
and the glory of my own authority

I could hardly let loose my hold,
could hardly contain the ecstatic
waves breaking against the walls
of my heart like crystal meth at

the joyful noise they made finally,
their gasps and sputterings of
praise . . . . And so I say unto you
of shallow faith, come down and drown

your sinful ways in the ordained
river of heaven. You can kick and
claw at the hand of the Almighty, but
you can't hold your breath forever.

The Flood

Yonder back of the house is a forest
where animals live I'll never learn to see

from here, from atop this deck I stick to
pretty closely mainly, because I built it

and because it gives me a certain point
of view on things I'm mostly apart from

anymore, things that are wild and dark
and strange and so I'm telling you this

by telling it to myself of course,
learning it as I go, as if this deck

were the deck of a ship – an ark say –
adrift in choppy, uncharted waters

rising every day; getting deeper that is;
that is, burying more and more of what,

now, I won't be going back to and who
can breathe water can choose not to stay.

Where I live is a flood plain on a shelf
a mile and more above a desert. North

is a volcano, and north of that a gash
so deep and long you could bury there

the entire citizenry of this town
and of a hundred others like it,

strip the bodies and stack them – laid out
head to toe – so as to compose a sort

of human shoal, a walkway for scrawny

*. . . and the Lord
said in his heart, I
will not again curse
the ground any
more for man's
sake; for the imagi-
nation of man's
heart is evil from
his youth; neither
will I again smite
any more every liv-
ing thing, as I have
done.*
– Genesis 8:21

73

animals to pick and feed their way along

when the rain comes thudding down on the land
like a horse carcass onto a face . . . .

It's an old story: how the world had to end
in human disaster or drown, instead,

that disaster in this disaster
it was promised would not happen again.

*F*rom here the trees look like masts of wrecked ships.
I used to run a dog among them; follow

as it followed the scent of something alive,
or once alive, or maybe just some hint

of weather building up behind the hills.
I had to trust senses keener than mine

to let myself range and climb to places
I knew I'd never return from alone.

What did I find? Once, this thing part rabbit,
part bird, noosed and dangling from a limb.

Once, the junked and love-stained back seat of a car.
Once, myself lost, the dog away, dark clouds

swimming overhead like the underbellies
of whales. Then the sky opened and I did

what I could: whistled twice for the dog, turned
up my collar and tacked into the gale.

*S*ay a dog buries a bone so deep
it can't find the scent to dig it up.

Say a brother buries a brother so hard

he becomes that brother – it can be like that.

Say everything you've ever cared about
and lost you've had to bury so many times

and ways you can't see straight anymore
into a cloud without seeing a face,

can't hear the rain without hearing a voice . . . .
With me it's the same. I have no choice

but to insist on the connectedness
of all this – the bone, the dog, the brothers, you

floating out there where I can't tow you in,
taking on water, learning to swim

face down: heart flush discarded for what
comes next, not back. The deck I cut.

*A*nd still the rain falls. The waters rise.
    I count the animals two by two –

the meek ones huddled against the storm;
the carnivores with their predatory eyes;

the ordinary, domestic beasts
for butchery or labor; the exotic

in which beauty has pronounced its own end;
the familiar; the companionable;

the winged and the wingless of the world –
and count myself single among them.

And ask myself what manner of creature
it is burrows so deeply into a place

it can never get out and will never

be found, and covers its eyes with its paws

and waits for however long it takes the flood
to subside and unbury the drowned.

I found what I could and led it on board,
but I couldn't find everything. And some

just didn't want to come, as though they knew
already how supplies would dwindle,

how the sun would hiss and wash from the sky,
how the ones that did survive, the elect,

would be kept on leashes thereafter,
or caged in zoos, or dissected in labs,

or hunted down anyway to extinction.
If each thing implies its opposite

then the living imply the dead. And what
was begun as a simple ship's log

has become this obituary instead.
How to recall them? – this one and this one –

all their kind through. How to forget them? – this one
and this one, and this one, and this one: you.

*F*or everything we can't put down
there's another thing we can't pick up.

For every hand we hold, now, another hand
we won't be dealt. For every story

that gets told through to an ending is
a different story we'll never get to hear,

or a different ending, or a different way
to arrive at that ending. There are

characters which, having advanced the plot,
will not again appear. You among them

I miss the most, whom I can't put down
however I try; though I'm alone here

on a deck in the world with the red sky
at morning and no stars all night, and take

what is given me given the story
I wrote myself into too far to unwrite . . . .

*T*he story I tell myself over
and over, the story I can't revise:

how once I believed that mercy was rain,
that rain was gentle, that the gentle

might rise above the flood tide of damage
visited upon them daily, that their lives

might float like a bottle with a message
of hope for someone else to find and read

someday; that the bottle would not break.
How far away I am from anything fixed

I have no way to know; nor the part I've played
in the harm that opens its widening fan,

like the wake of this vessel, across
the face of the earth. All I know is

a voice in my head said *Prepare for the worst.*
Save what you can. And I believed it.

*J*im Simmerman's previous books of poetry
include *Home*, picked by Raymond Carver as a
Pushcart "Writer's Choice" selection; *Once Out of
Nature*, a "Best of the Small Presses" book exhibit
at the Frankfurt Book Fair; and *Moon Go Away, I
Don't Love You No More*, nominated for the
Pulitzer Prize and the National Book Award. He
co-edited *Dog Music: Poetry about Dogs*. His
poems have appeared in such places as *Antaeus,
Poetry, Pushcart Prize X*, and he has received fel-
lowships from the National Endowment for the
Arts, the Arizona Commission on the Arts, the
Provincetown Fine Arts Work Center, and the
Hawthornden Castle International Retreat for
Writers. A former Secretary and Board member
of Associated Writing Programs, he lives in the
high country of northern Arizona.